Trophy of Grace

The Prayer Advocate's Encounter with The Unknown-COVID-19

D1285652

Trophy of Grace

The Prayer Advocate's Encounter with The Unknown-COVID-19

Anita Johnson Merchant

Dedication

This book is dedicated to all those who have survived COVID-19.

To all those who lost their lives to COVID-19.

To all those who lost a loved one to COVID-19 and are grieving the loss.

To all the front-line workers who took a chance with their lives to care during the unknown of COVID-19.

In Loving Memory

In memory of my niece, Shanndolyn Shernett Turner, a front-line worker whose life was too short on this earth.

"Trophy of Grace"

Psalm 91: 14-16 (GW)

"Because you love me, I will rescue you.

I will protect you because you know my name.

When you call to me, I will answer you.

I will be with you when you are in trouble.

I will save you and honor you.

I will satisfy you with a long life.

I will show you how I will save you."

Colossians 4:2 (NLT)

"Devote yourselves to prayer with an alert mind and a thankful heart."

TABLE OF CONTENTS

INTRODUCTION

The Prayer Advocate

As a Certified Prayer Intercessor, prayer is at the forefront. It is taught. It is the action one comes to understand that must be done. Having been praying for many years, the focus is always on how to go to God on others' behalf. Keep in mind Intercessors are key people who intercede to God on others' behalf. Intercessors tend to put themselves last even on their own prayer list or go to God in prayer on their own behalf.

Having been anointed to pray for others at a young age, I started to understand the power of prayer. Over the years of understanding the power of prayer and why it is so important to have a consistent prayer life, a motto was developed — "I am SOLD OUT TO PRAYER."

Knowing the power of prayer, praying for others, knowing prayer is the most powerful tool God gave his people to fight against the enemy; however, prayer does not exempt one from suffering. It simply cannot be escaped.

Encountering COVID-19 was my time of suffering. Yes, a devoted Intercessor could not escape! Many may think it was because of sin or something I did to encounter COVID-19 as the reasoning behind contracting the virus. It truly may never be known except by our Creator. Either way, I am grateful that God knows the how and why.

1 Peter 5:10 (NIV) "And the God of all grace, who called you to his eternal glory in Christ, after you have suffered a little while, will himself restore you and make you strong, firm, and steadfast."

While reading this book, I pray that you develop an understanding resulting in a different perspective knowing no one is exempt from suffering. It's a part of the human experience. This journey happens to be about a Prayer Intercessor "SOLD OUT TO PRAYER" who God made His "Trophy of Grace."

1

SUFFERING WILL COME-EMBRACE IT

People tend to believe, especially Christians, because we serve the Lord, claim to be saved, go to church every Sunday, and with other things proclaimed to honor God, tend to question God when there is a time to suffer in our lives. The truth about grace is we are saved by grace through faith.

Having sustainable faith as an Intercessor was tested during my encounter with COVID-19. Throughout the suffering, there were many moments of "faithlessness," "great faith," and times of "little faith. The Holy Spirit would remind me of my little faith when I would begin to worry, be fearful, and allow doubt to sink into my thoughts.

Hebrews 11:6 (NIV) "And without faith it is impossible to please God because anyone who comes to him must believe that he exists and that he rewards those who earnestly seek him."

Speaking to the mountain, also known as the problem, is what had to be done to demonstrate my faith. It required not going to God in prayer about the problem but speaking directly to COVID-19. Speak to the aching, speak to the chills, speak to the fever, speak to the illusions, speak to the loss of taste, speak to the loss of smell, speak to grasping for breath, speak to the poor appetite, speak to struggling to walk, speak to not being able to sleep, speak to the headaches, and speak to the feeling of helplessness. Tapping into the authority given by God, knowing whose he said I was in Christ, using the word of God, the name of Jesus), the healer, and the Holy Spirit to stop the devil's attack on my body.

The story of Job gives an account or reminds me of my encounter with COVID-19. God allowed COVID-19 to take over my entire body. I have come to understand nothing happens without God's permission. "NOTHING."

We all have been given a measure of faith. It is up to us to use it according to the authority given by God.

Knowing faith was the only thing that would sustain me, my confidence and trust in God was not going to be based just on what I saw but based on what I had already seen God do. I had to lean into the faith Jesus had already deposited into my Spirit. I HAD TO EMBRACE THE SUFFERING. So, I continued to speak over myself. I continued to read and search the word of God about suffering.

God intends for our faith and our actions to go hand in hand. There has to be belief first. Even with whatever kind of suffering being encountered, even what it looks like with the physical eye or what the body is feeling, your belief is what sustains you.

The thoughts of "great faith" would automatically surface from within when there were signs of a turnaround. But the days I was actually not seeing or how the body was actually feeling, "little faith" would try and creep into my Spirit. This faith thing was easy to believe when days were good, while the relatively bad days took a lot more praying and so much more faith.

I share all of this to remind you how someone SOLD OUT TO PRAYER also had to endure a time of suffering.

You may ponder the question, "Why did The Prayer Advocate faith waver at times? Did she forget how God brought her out of previous trials?" A time of suffering brings out all kinds of thoughts and emotions.

Even in the midst of the suffering, I continued to intercede for others and also interjected parts of my time praying for myself. I have grown in knowledge and experience. Taking your mind and eyes off your own time of suffering makes your suffering seem minimum.

Sharing my encounter with COVID-19 encourages those who have witnessed others suffering who were not given grace with their encounter. Grace is not something we can earn or purchase. Grace is only given by God. He decides who will receive His Grace.

Ask yourself these 3 questions:

- Are there encounters going on in life motivating faith?

- Is there a need to re-evaluate faith?

- Is faith the substance?

While moving forward reading about my encounter with COVID-19, I pray your faith becomes stronger than ever before. When a time of suffering comes, knowing through faith His grace is sufficient, and you will have your own Trophy of Grace or witness someone else's Trophy of Grace.

2 Corinthians 12:9 (NIV) But he said to me, "My grace is sufficient for you, for my power is made perfect in weakness. "Therefore, I will boast all the more gladly about my weaknesses, so that Christ's power may rest on me."

Breathe Moment

God is with us every step of the way. He is willing to do whatever it takes. Just have faith!

2

TROUBLES OF THE WORLD-A PANDEMIC

As an Intercessor, when things start to attack the land, prompted by the Holy Spirit, he leads Intercessors into praying immediately. A gathering of groups or individually began to pray specifically in order to get a breakthrough.

There was no definitive information at the beginning of COVID-19. The virus hit the land like an uncontrollable wave. As most would say, it came without any warning. From the name of the virus to its impact on the world, it was unimaginable.

When COVID-19 began to sweep across the US, it brought the US and the entire world to a standstill. This actually took over the entire world immediately, causing fear to set in. When the world was first notified about COVID-19, many did not perceive it as an emergency until a world-breaking number of people started rapidly dying. The medical world was not sure of what was occurring but knew from what they saw that it was not something they had dealt with before. Can you begin to imagine the fear that was upon them? COVID-19 was spreading at such a rapid pace that hospitals and clinics were flooding with people experiencing problems with breathing and or shortness of breath. People were also complaining of many other combined symptoms. The medical world didn't really understand how COVID-19 was being contracted. They didn't even really know where to start or how to start treating patients to get the virus under control. Sidebar, most people do not handle the unknown very well. Can you begin to imagine the fear that was within the medical people and what they may have been thinking? Can you imagine the anxiety that came upon them? The worry, the frustration, and most of all wondering if they would contract the virus?

I believe it takes a person who has some type of belief in God to be steadfast and unmovable to stay the course even knowing it could possibly cause them death.

Keep in mind these words: the unknown. While reading this book, you can testify you have experienced "the unknown." There is no way humanly possible around experiencing the unknown. It is what it is, the unknown. Think about the feelings that come about when experiencing those moments. Just imagine, at the same time, it could involve life or death. The mind can only speculate, having not experienced this.

2 Corinthians 16:9 (NASB) "For the eyes of the Lord move to and from throughout the earth that He may strongly support those whose heart is completely His."

What Is Covid-19?

To my understanding, COVID-19 is caused by a coronavirus called SARS-CoV-2. This type of coronavirus was never seen before. COVID-19 was found to be contracted through contact with another person who had the virus and or released into the air. It is predominantly a respiratory illness that can also affect other organs. A diagnosis of COVID-19 has a wide range of symptoms ranging from mild symptoms to severe illnesses. Symptoms appeared 2 to 14 days after exposure to the virus: fever, chills, cough, shortness of breath, fatigue, muscle, and body aches, loss of taste, smell, sore throat, congestion, runny nose, and nausea, vomiting, and diarrhea.

Just reading all of the symptoms along will bring fear upon a person. For we all know how important it is to breathe. I am going to drop this right here. When you think about it, who do you know could shut the entire United States down, nonetheless, the entire world. Each continent was blaming China. Even though that may be where it possibly started, no continent, place, person or thing can really be blamed. Why am I sharing this? Where COVID-19 started should not really be the concern. How it affected the world should always be the concern. The number of people who lost their lives and had an encounter with COVID-19 and survived should also be of concern.

We hear the term we have to stay ready and not have to get ready. Well, the world was not ready for COVID-19. The number of people who died is evident of that. Many didn't have time to get ready to protect themselves. On March 11, 2020, COVID-19 was announced to the world mainly due to the rapid number of people dying. The rate people were dying and the world having to deal with something it was not prepared for was unspeakable. I can go on and on about the beginning and how it rapidly affected so many people worldwide, but the story of how it came about is just the beginning.

When we look at how it started, it's painful for me. Sometimes I find myself having a conversation asking God what was He really trying to do? We can speculate and come up with all kinds of conclusions. As a Christian, I have come to several conclusions. I really cannot definitively say. I came up with my own conclusion, which was-God took a drastic measure to get the world's attention. The virus was not isolated to a place or person. Your race did not matter. Your bank account did not matter. Even your title didn't matter. It's hard to put a single word or reason on the world experiencing COVID-19. We have heard so many people's perspectives. Yes, that's exactly what we all can do, have our own individual perspective.

The world was at a standstill. I asked God, "Now what, Lord?" Even with the world shut down, there was one thing God did connect to him keeping his promises. Provisions were still tagged along with COVID-19. Meaning, with all the shortages of things needed-paper towels, toilet paper, hand sanitizing, anti-bacteria wipes, God still provided. A conversation could go back and forth in our minds; however, every human was part of the COVID-19 plan when it's all said and done.

Over the months of healing from COVID-19, a belief of God allowing what He wants, and he does it the way He wants. Just that simple. God chooses what, who, when, how long, and where an encounter occurs in one's life. As an Intercessor, my prayers include asking God to help me accept his will or help whom I am praying for to accept his will. For His plan will prevail. It's not that I didn't believe this prior to my encounter with COVID-19. It's because God let me survive (showed me GRACE)-His plan to share with the world. That is exactly what I am doing within the pages of this book.

Isaiah 41:10 (NIV)

"So do not fear, for I am with you; do not be dismayed, for I am your God. I will strengthen you and help you; I will uphold you with my righteous right hand."

Breathe Moment

Knowing God is the Father of compassion and the power of prayer gives just enough hope to look to the Father.

3

ENCOUNTERING THE UNKNOWN

As humans, we want to know the unknown. Something about our nature results in being that way. We want to know what, when, where, why, and how. Knowing all these things in advance will help us be better prepared. Knowing in advance allows us to develop a plan and put things in place for whatever challenge is forthcoming. It also does not allow fear to take the lead seat.

Knowing who God is and having many hours studying His Word, He knows that experiencing the unknown is part of life. Knowing who God is and seeing his marvelous works, you would think one would not even concern themselves about the unknown. From studying His Word, you would think that one would do exactly what His Word says.

Proverbs 3:5 (NIV) "Trust in the Lord with all your heart and lean not onto your own understanding."

There are numerous times in one's life, this is hard to do. We can all testify to this. We do and even quote this scripture until we encounter the unknown. I am speaking from experience.

The beginning of the encounter with COVID-19 started off while living in New Orleans, Louisiana. At that time, the cities rate of infectious people was high compared to the rest of the world. I had my morning devotion time, one cup of coffee, exercised, and felt like I was on top of the world. I had listened to my motivating songs while preparing myself to go into the office. I drove to the office at my regular time to report by 9:30 a.m. When I left my home, there was no reason to even think about the unknown. I made it into the office and continued with my usual routine of checking in with the team, headed to my office, and logging onto our agency system. Nothing out of the unusual happened. As time went on that day around NOON, I began to feel a little achy, and my throat began to feel sore. I didn't think anything of it because I had not been sick prior to it. I proceeded to take some over-the-counter medication for flu-like cold systems as I had done in the past when feeling flu-like or cold symptoms.

I proceeded to stay in the office and continued to work, thinking whatever it was, it would pass. I began to drink some hot tea an hour later, thinking it would surely help. It seemed to always help in the past. Around 2:00 pm, I began to feel worse, but I ignored the symptoms and thought to myself it would pass once I got home, shower, take additional medication and get to bed early. It would surely be all over the next morning. Around 4:00 p.m., the symptoms were worse, and now at this point, I was beginning to ache all over. So, I automatically assumed I was coming down with the flu.

By that time, I was the closing manager and the only Manger on duty, so I had to stay at the office until 6:00 p.m. to lock the office and set the alarm. By 6:00 p.m., I felt like something had come over me like a quick wave. I had taken over-the-counter daytime flu medication earlier, so I drank another cup of hot tea prior to leaving the office.

Preparing to leave the office, I began to pray. After leaving the office, while driving, I began to speak to the Lord, you know how we Christians do. "Lord, whatever is attacking my body, I declare and decree it will not overtake my body." I went directly home, not stopping anywhere while en route to home. I was able to make it home safely. Once I made it into the apartment, I began to believe all would be well.

I proceeded to my bedroom, putting all the items I had in hand in its designated place, grabbing my pajamas, and headed directly to the bathroom to shower. While showering, I could feel something taking over my body, which I had never felt before.

Being The Prayer Advocate and sold out to prayer, of course, I began to pray to God, asking Him to help with whatever was going on with my body. I began to speak to God, asking Him to allow his healing power to remove whatever had attacked my body and give me wisdom as to what was going on with my body. I had experienced the flu before, and I knew it was more to the symptoms than the flu. I was experiencing symptoms I had never encountered before. The magnitude of the aches, chills, the pain started to be severe. I remember crying out to God, asking him to help me. The pain began to decrease. I managed to get out of the shower and get dressed for bed. On my way to the bedroom, I glanced at the clock. It was 8:00 p.m. I got into bed, and I said thank you, Lord, for letting me make it to the bed. At that point, all I wanted to do was lay down, thinking once I got rest overnight, all would be fine in the morning.

Being alone, you really tend to call on Jesus more frequently than if you had someone with you. I began to pray to God: "Lord, you know all things. I cry out to you and ask you to remove whatever is attacking my body. Lord, you have the power to do so. Send me one of your healing angels. Lord, I don't know what it is, but I know I have to trust you. Lord, I am feeling something all over my body like never before." You see, when I pray, I pray specific prayers. I got out of bed to get some water because I was beginning to be extremely thirsty. I returned to bed and eventually drifted off to sleep.

I glanced at the clock in the middle of the night; it was around 4:00 am. I was awakened due to having problems breathing. It started to get worse. I became afraid. I immediately started to call out Jesus' name. Holy Spirit spoke and said, "Call 911." I reached for my cell phone. I began to really struggle to breathe, and at that point, I really was afraid due to being alone. When alone and experiencing a health issue, fear creeps in, and your mind starts to wonder all kinds of what-ifs and immediately tells you to seek help.

After calling 911, the operator took the call and followed the protocol of asking for my personal information. While answering her questions, she could hear me gasping to breathe. I told her I was alone and afraid. She spoke in a calm tone, managing to keep me calm, and informed me she was sending an ambulance and she would stay on the phone until the ambulance arrived. She instructed me to see if I could walk and go and unlock the door so the paramedics could get inside the apartment. I managed to unlock the door and make it back to the bed. So much was going through my mind while I waited. The 911 operator continued to speak with me until the paramedics arrived.

The paramedics arrived and proceeded to attend to me. I told them I was having problems breathing. They continue to work on checking things out. I was then given oxygen by a tube. After being placed in the ambulance, all I did was silently start to pray. All I could think about was did I have COVID-19. After seeing the news the day before, starting to feel ill that included the symptoms, I continued to pray all the way while traveling to the hospital. It was such a lonely ride. I had not ridden in an ambulance since my youngest son was 2, who is now in his twenties. So, imagine how scared I was. The unknown of what was attacking my body, having not been inside an ambulance for over 20 years and physically alone besides those who were assisting me.

Now being The Prayer Advocate, the thought of being alone should have been far from my mind. God keeps his promises.

Philippians 4:9 (NIV) "Whatever you have learned or received or heard from me or seen in me put it into practice. And the God of peace will be with you."

Yes, I knew His Word, but at that time of not knowing the unknown, I must say the feeling of being close to God at that time I was losing the feeling of closeness to God.

After arriving at the hospital and being taken inside, the paramedics alerted the hospital staff. I was then rolled into the hallway, where I waited to be seen. The hospital was cold, dreary, and there was no one except the hospital staff inside. All the chairs were taped off. Anyone I was able to see had their mask on. You could hear a pin drop. It was so quiet. I was moved into one of the emergency room treatment rooms. The medical staff checked my temperature, blood pressure, etc.

After answering questions, I was connected to an IV and continued with oxygen at the same time. I was there for a couple of hours. It seemed like forever. I began to feel somewhat better. At that point, I thought I was going to receive the COVID-19 test, especially since I was complaining of problems with breathing. The ER doctor and nurse returned, and the doctor proceeded to inform me I didn't have a high enough temp or all the symptoms to be given a COVID-19 test.

The hospital had limited tests, nor were they going to admit me due to the limit of beds available. I was given instructions, if the symptoms continue, to contact my primary doctor. I remained quiet. Let me inform you this was a weekend, to be specific, a Saturday morning. We all know to contact a primary doctor on a weekend is unheard of. The nurse proceeded to remove the IV and other things connected. She left the room and came back with discharge papers. Now keep in mind I rode alone in the ambulance to the hospital. So, therefore, I did not have a ride back to my apartment. The question may cross your mind why didn't I call someone to pick me up? It was 4:00 am, and I lived in the city with no family. Now I could have called a friend, but I allowed my pride to keep me from doing so. That pride thing is something I struggle with. I ordered an UBER- I had built a friendship with a nice lady after using her service as an UBER driver who told me to call whenever I needed a ride.

Walking through the emergency room was like walking through a cold freezer with no one in sight. I looked for the exit door. There was a path mapped out on the wall and floor you had to follow to exit. I followed the path and ended up at a window with a lady sitting behind it who spoke through the window, informing me I didn't need to do anything else. While turning to go towards the exit door, I observed all the seats were tapped off, and a guard was sitting at the entrance to the exit door. He just stared. I walked out to the street area, and the UBER had arrived.

Upon arriving back to the apartment, I entered and immediately undressed and showered. I was feeling somewhat better. I believe it was from having the oxygen and IV fluids. I went to bed and was able to sleep through the night.

Upon waking up the following morning, I began to start aching again, coughing returned, and I began to sweat. I began to drink orange juice and take what I had at home to help with the symptoms. I manage to get a piece of toast down for breakfast. Continuing to feel the flu-like symptoms, I decided to go back to bed.

As I lay in bed, I began to talk to God, "Lord, what is going on with my body?" I held on to the fact he healed my 2-year-old son from cancer. There was no doubt in my mind of his healing power. I conversed with God until I dozed off to sleep. I recall that it was on a Thursday, and I continued to stay in bed through the weekend. By Sunday, I started having problems breathing again and asked, "Lord, what shall I do?" Holy Spirit nudged me to get medical help. All I thought about was how I saw on the news how people were rapidly dying. I refused to die alone in my apartment. After my experience at the emergency room, I thought I would try another source. I decided to go to Urgent Care.

I managed to throw on some sweats and drove 3 miles to the closest location from where I lived. Upon arrival, I completed paperwork, etc., waited in the lobby for about 15 minutes. The nurse called me back. She was dressed in protective gear and wearing a mask. She proceeded to take my temperature. It registered I had a fever. The nurse asked me how long I had been feeling bad and to describe my symptoms.

After the discussion, she stated she was going to give me a flu test. The results of the test came back negative for the flu. She went on to say the clinic did not have the COVID-19 test. She went on to say I would need to go to the ER for a COVID-19 test. I informed her I had already been to the ER and was told I could not get the test because I did not have all the major systems. She then went on to ask what pharmacy I used because she was going to call in two prescriptions and give me a note for work. I concluded she knew I was ill but was unsure what it was and did not know how to treat the symptoms we discussed since the flu test came back negative.

I proceeded to exit the exam room and go towards the exit door. I exited the clinic and walked to my Jeep. I could barely walk to get into my vehicle. I couldn't go and get the medication due to the pharmacy not being opened so early. It was before 9:00 a.m. on a Sunday. I could barely drive but managed to drive back to my apartment. After arriving home, I began to pray and ask God what was going on with my body. I plead to him to help me, to give me wisdom on what to do next. I got in bed and just laid there. I had bottled water by my bed and began to drink it. I began to breathe better as long as I was sitting up, so I managed to prop pillows behind my head to sit upward. I eventually dozed off to sleep again, mainly because I was exhausted from being up throughout the previous night. When I woke up, I was extremely wet. I got up and changed into some fresh sweats. By this time, the pharmacy was opened. I got the two prescriptions hoping I was going to get better. What I was experiencing, the feeling would pass once I got the medications. I began to pray again, "Lord, you know what I need. You know what is attacking my body. Please provide the opportunity for me to get the assistance I need."

I was extremely weak but was determined to get the medication.

Even when going through a trial, we can still be tested while in the trial. I arrive safely at the pharmacy driving to the drive-thru window, you know the drill. After giving the information, I was told the prescription was not ready, and it would be about 15 minutes. She asked if I could come inside to prevent holding up the drive-thru line. Now you know what we do. I said, "Ok," but while driving off, I said, "The devil is a liar; I am getting the medications."

I probably should have continued my prayer -conversation with God instead of giving the enemy any acknowledgment. We as Christians are quick to give the enemy credit when it could be God testing our faith. I am sure many who are reading this can relate.

At this point, people had not been made afraid of being around others. The world was still operating as usual. And also, at that time I wasn't even aware I had COVID-19. I just knew something was not right with my body, especially how I was feeling.

I waited and received the two prescriptions. I returned back home. I immediately took the mediations, showered again, and went to bed. Slept the entire day. When I woke up, it was evening time. My clothing was wet, so I assumed it was because of the fever. I decided to shower, assuming that would make me feel better.

For the next three days, I stayed in bed only to get out of bed when it was absolutely necessary. The days and nights seemed so long. Yet, I still was not getting better. Sitting up in bed because I found myself breathing better without feeling as though I was suffocating. When I would try and lay down, it was as if I was underwater, gasping for air.

My niece called me, and I shared with her how bad I was feeling. She immediately became concerned. She had been watching the news. She even made the comment I didn't sound well. I began to share with her what I had done thus far. She went on to say how crazy it all sounded, and she hated I had to experience all those things just to get medical care.

After ending my conversation with her, I began to pray.

Zephaniah 3: 16-17 (MSG) "Don't be afraid. Dear Zion, don't despair. Your God is present among you, a strong Warrior there to save you. Happy to have you back, he'll calm you with his love and delight you with his songs."

Breathe Moment

Life can be different when we breathe each breath, knowing God is right with us every step of the way.

4

IF FIRST YOU DON'T SUCCEED-
GUIDE ME HOLY SPIRIT

I woke up in the middle of the day gasping for breath. It frightened me so much! I began to speak to God. "Lord, help me-what should I do." The Holy Spirit spoke and said, "Go back to the ER." I knew I was not able to drive. I did not hesitate to call 911.

Psalm 34:4 (NIV) "I sought the Lord, and he answered me, he delivered me from all my fears."

I went through the normal protocol answering questions, and again, the dispatcher told me she was sending the ambulance. The paramedics arrived and noticed how my breathing was not normal. They proceeded to put the oxygen mask on my face and proceeded to take me to the ambulance. Upon route to the hospital, I was asked a series of questions while the paramedics continued to assist me. I was asked which hospital I wanted to go to. Of course, I dare not go back to the first hospital that sent me home. I silently asked God for his wisdom, and he vividly spoke.

Isaiah 41:13 (MSG) "That's right, Because I, your God, have a firm grip on you and I'm not letting go. I'm telling you, Don't panic. I'm right here to help you."

I told them a different hospital. Upon arriving at a different hospital, I was transported to an area where all patients arriving were taken with breathing problems. I was then placed in a chair and told someone would be with me as soon as a doctor or nurse was available. Now keep in mind I was receiving oxygen while in the ambulance.

The oxygen was removed while I sat in the waiting area. I patiently sat waiting. It seemed the wait was extremely long. I assumed that since I was not gasping for my breath, it was no longer an emergency to the hospital staff.

Finally, my name was called. A doctor approached me. She gave me a test to check my oxygen level. The results did not reflect an oxygen level problem. She informed me they could not give me the COVID-19 test because I did not have all of the symptoms, but she would order some fluids to give me through an IV and observe me. She didn't feel I needed to be admitted to the hospital. A gentleman proceeded to take me in a wheelchair to the back ER area and preceded to assist me into bed. Vital signs were taken, and the IV was connected. He suggested I try and rest because I would be there for a while until the IV was complete.

I remember dosing off to sleep. Upon waking up, I noticed it was much later. The nurse enters the room. The IV had been completed. She asked how I was feeling. She said my temperature was down, and my oxygen level was good. She disconnected the IV and asked if I had someone to call to pick me up. Immediately the Holy Spirit spoke to me and said to call my friend Charlain. I responded to the nurse, informing her I did. I called Charlain, and she informed me she would be there to pick me up. While waiting for her, the Holy Spirit nudged me to call my family back home once I got back to the apartment to inform them of what was going on.

Holy Spirit spoke:

Isaiah 41:10 (NIV) "So do not fear, for God is with you; do not be dismayed, for He is your God. He will strengthen me and help me; He will uphold me with his righteous right hand."

Thank God for the Holy Spirit!

I was released from the ER. I was told to inform the person picking me up to let me know when they arrived because no one could come into the hospital, someone from within the hospital would take me out in a wheelchair. Once Charlain alerted me of her arrival, I informed her of the area I would be. I was pushed by an attendant by wheelchair to the door, and I proceeded to walk out to her car. Charlain made sure I got home safely inside and told me to call her if I needed anything else.

I still was not feeling well. Within the next few days, I started to really feel bad again. By this time, my sisters had traveled to my home to see what was really going on after I shared with them what I had already experienced.

After staying a few days, I started feeling worst, and my sisters became concerned. They were communicating with our older sister, who lived in Ohio. She informed them to have me call my primary doctor and alert her of what was going on.

I proceeded to call the doctor's office, explaining to the nurse assistant what was going on and what I had done thus far. The doctor immediately returned my call. After hearing me speak over the telephone explaining what was going on, what I had already done, the two ER visits by ambulance, with an Urgent Care visit in between. She asked if I was given the COVID-19 test. I informed her I was only given the flu test, and it came back negative. She immediately said she was going to have her nurse call in several prescriptions. She instructed me to drink plenty of water to stay hydrated. If I didn't feel any better in a couple of days after taking the medications, she asked that I call her back.

Lamentations 3:57 (ESV) "You came near when I called on you; you said, "Do not fear!"

Keep in mind that the medical field was still trying to find out information about COVID-19. How to treat the virus, what was causing the virus to spread so quickly, how to prevent catching the virus. They were afraid of the unknown. The hospitals were only giving tests to those with severe symptoms due to the lack of tests. There was a serious lack of tests available. There was a shortage of supplies and hospital rooms.

My sisters decided one of them would stay while the others went back home. A few days had gone by. I didn't feel any better. In the middle of the night after the 3rd day of taking the prescriptions, I began to experience breathing as if I was suffocating. I became so afraid. I called out to my sister. She came to the bedroom and also became frightened. Holy Spirit nudged me to call 911.

I dialed 911 and cried out to the dispatcher, telling her I had problems breathing. She could hear the struggle in my voice. I was crying and trying to talk at the same time. She began to speak calmly to me to calm me down. I informed her it was my third time calling 911 and that I was sent back home each of the previous two times. I told her no one believed me each time I told them I had difficulty breathing. At this point, I was hysterical. She informed me an ambulance was en route. She remained on the phone, trying to calm me.

All kinds of thoughts were going through my mind. I had seen the news where thousands of people were dying daily from COVID-19. I could see in my sisters' eyes how afraid she was. Yet still, up to this point, we were not sure if I had contracted the virus due to not having been tested. I began to calm down once I started praying and saying:

Psalm 23:4 (KJV) "Yea though I walk through the valley of the shallow of death, I will fear no evil, for thou art with me; thy rod and thy staff, they comfort me."

This was the third time the Holy Spirit instructed me to call 911 and return to the ER. The paramedics arrived. They could see I was gasping for breath and proceeded to assist me. One of the paramedics commented, asking the question, "Didn't an ambulance come to this resident before?" I just nodded my head yes. So, they proceeded again to take me to the hospital.

2 Corinthians 4:8-10 (ESV) "We are afflicted in every way, but not crushed; perplexed, but not driven to despair; persecuted, but not forsaken; struck down, but not destroyed; always carrying in the body the death of Jesus, so that the life of Jesus may also be manifested in our bodies."

Breathe Moment

No matter when and how you encounter a time of suffering, God will give you what you need at the exact time of your need.

5

ENTERING A DUNGEON

Arriving at the ER, I was immediately taken to a room. I was placed on the ER bed. A doctor and several nurses were in the room. Things were being attached to me. I began to be asked a series of questions. Had I had the COVID-19 test? How long had I been feeling bad? Describe my symptoms? From that point, things began to shift. A discussion between a doctor and another staff person references the test went like this:

Doctor: "Order the COVID-19 test."

Staff person: "But she does not have all the symptoms to qualify for the test."

Doctor: "This is the patient's third time coming to ER for the symptoms she mentions. I don't care. Order the test."

At that point, I knew God was shifting things.

Philippians 4:6 (NIV) "Do not be anxious about anything, but in every situation, by prayer and petition with thanksgiving, present your requests to God."

Staff person: "Not sure if we have a bed for her."

I began to cry. At that time, my sister was calling my cell phone. I was able to answer and inform her they would be sending me back home.

Psalm 61:1-2 (NIV) "Hear my cry, O God; listen to my prayer. From the ends of the earth, I call to you, I call as my heart grows faint; lead me to the rock that is higher than I."

Doctor: "Ms. Merchant, we are going to admit you. Tell your family member someone will be calling as soon as I get you admitted with the necessary protocol." My sister heard the doctor and said, "Okay."

I was finally admitted to the hospital. The doctor explained to me the possibility of having to go on a ventilator. He said he had to have my permission just in case I could not give the ok later. I began to cry, he began to share encouraging words, "don't worry, Ms. Merchant, we are going to up the oxygen first before even considering a ventilator. If your body starts to accept the oxygen, you won't need a ventilator."

Immediately I began to moan and groan.

Romans 8:28 (NIV) "In the same way, the Spirit helps us in our weakness. We do not know what we ought to pray for, but the Spirit himself intercedes for us through wordless groans."

After a while, the room was not occupied by any hospital staff. I was alone. While staring at the ceiling, tears were flowing down my face. I spoke into the atmosphere, "God, surely you are not going to take me out like this!" I recalled God's word telling me I could go boldly to him. I could speak my true thoughts. I could remind him of what His Word said.

1 John 5:14-15 (NIV) "This is the confidence we have in approaching God: that if we ask anything according to his will, he hears us. And if we know that he hears us whatever, we ask-we know that we have what we asked of him."

Anytime I am faced with difficulties, my mind always recalls this,

"It's our birthright to pray with confidence in our heavenly Father's ability to intervene in any situation. He wants us to pray with boldness and courage-not because we have it all together, but rather that He holds it all together with us in mind." Crystal McDowell

A nurse entered the room and said they were moving me to ICU. While being rolled to the elevator, I began to recall while I was at home listening to the news, many people who went to that hospital ward were not returning home. Immediately there was a dreary feeling when the elevator doors opened to the ICU floor. Keep in mind there was no one except hospital personnel at the hospital during this time. Each person was covered from their head to their feet. You could only see their eyes. The eyes glared a picture of fear. You know that look when someone is afraid. There were no smiles to be seen or really any talking going on unless it was necessary. The eyes tell a lot, especially when words are not spoken.

I was rolled into my assigned room and placed onto the bed. Shortly after, a nurse came into the room, of course, standing at a distance covered from her head to her feet. She introduced herself. She went on to explain she would be my nurse for the night. I nodded my head to acknowledge that I could hear her. She took my vitals.

I was so exhausted from not getting rest at home due to listening making sure I was breathing. I had been sleeping, sitting up in the bed to breathe. The last thing I remembered seeing was the nurse leaving the room, and I fell asleep.

When I woke up, I glanced up, and the TV clock showed 4:00 a.m. I was confused and began to look around. I really could not move very much. I was cold and thirsty. My body was still aching. I said, "God, please send a healing angel to this room." And I went back to sleep.

Upon waking up, at this point, I had lost track of what day it was and felt like I was just lying in a place of unknown. The room was cold and dreary. The only light was the light from the TV and from the bottom of the door reflecting from the hallway. There was a night light that shined from within the bathroom. You could hear a pin drop. It was just that quiet.

One of the days, while the nurse was checking my vitals, she mentioned that the COVID-19 test had come back positive. Tears began to flow. She said, "You are going to be alright. Your body is accepting the oxygen." She smiled and said other nurses mentioned I was really moaning in my sleep. She said, "Baby," with that New Orleans accent-which I adore, "I told them that patient is talking to God." I smiled and began to stop crying.

The days started blending into the nights. I could see outside the two windows in the room. The daylight and the sunlight gave me hope each morning I saw the sunrise. I lost track of how many days I had been in the hospital. I began to feel really down. My mind was all over the place with what-ifs. One of those mornings, I glance out of the two windows, and from out of nowhere, a white dove landed on the window siding. Made the sound doves make and flew away. Tears began to flow down my face. I smiled and thought God had not forgotten about me.

You only saw a nurse when it was time for vitals. There were times I would hear feet running and the words "code blue" to room (whatever the room number was). I felt my pulse rising and the monitor going off. The nurse came into my room and assured me I was ok and to try and keep calm. Those were just calls to assist others.

When she exited the room, I began to open my mouth and say, "There will be no code blue for this room; I declare and decree I would leave the hospital and go home." I started calling on the name of Jesus. I began to remind the Lord of what he said in His Word. "Lord, you said you are my healer. You have all power to do anything. Nothing is too hard for you."

Each time I heard code blue over the intercom, I would remind God of his promises. I would even pray for the person by the room number. I even prayed for the staff-I could hear some of them crying in the hallway.

Even though I was speaking to God daily, dark thoughts would creep into my mind just for a moment. There were sometimes hours when I would speak to those thoughts.

Psalm 119:105 (NIV) "Your word is a lamp for my feet, a light on my path."

Holy Spirit would constantly remind me of God's healing power. He would often speak to me not to give up. One night I was in such a dark place. I wept for hours, asking God, "Why me? What did I do wrong? I am a clean person. I need to be here on earth to see my granddaughter grow up through her life. Why are you allowing me to suffer? I am The Prayer Advocate who is sold out to prayer. Why me, why me, Lord?" Somehow, I just cried myself to sleep.

When I woke up the next morning, I was staring at the TV. It was on mute. I really tried hard not to look at too much TV. I was getting depressed seeing the number of people who had died, who were hospitalized, how families could not go and see their loved ones, how nurses were using their cell phones to dial loved ones to say goodbye to their loved ones before dying. I had not communicated with my family for several days due to my cell phone needing to be charged. I didn't have a charger, and besides, the hospital staff wanted me to get much rest. The nurse would inform me they had spoken to my family, and my family had been calling.

On that day in the afternoon, the doctor and nurse came to my room and said they had turned down my oxygen level the night before while

I was sleeping to see if my body would breathe ok on its own. She said things went well. She then said the oxygen was going to be removed the rest of the day to see how my breathing was without any oxygen. The doctor said if my breathing showed no problems and I continued to breathe on my own, especially through the night, she would consider me going home. I started crying. The nurse shared encouraging words. The doctor smiled and said, "You are a miracle, especially not having to go on the ventilator." I held my tears in and smiled.

When the two of them departed the room, I began to praise God!!!!! I had to calm myself down because I could see the machine numbers rising. You ever had to praise God in a quiet way, where you can't scream, but you can just whisper and know that God hears you. Well, that is exactly how I had to praise him at that moment.

The nurse returned and slowly removed the oxygen tube from my nose. I must admit I was nervous about whether I would be able to breathe on my own. I was still holding on to the feelings I had when I couldn't breathe. The nurse walked me through a breathing process as she was removing the oxygen. I began to relax, and it went well. I thanked her, and she said she was overjoyed to see me breathe and excited that I would possibly go home tomorrow. She said I was a blessing and gave the nurses hope. Instead of rolling me out in a body bag, I would be rolled out in a wheelchair.

All I could say to her was, "God is still good!" She replied, "ALL THE TIME." I told her I had also prayed for them because they were putting their lives in danger to care for those of us with COVID-19. She thanked me.

Throughout the rest of the day, I prayed and slept, prayed, and slept. When evening time had come, it dawned on me I was really breathing on my own. I thanked God again and again.

Psalm 30:2 (NASB) "O Lord my God, I cried to You for help, and You healed me."

The evening nurse came into the room to check my vitals. All were good. She said the doctor spoke with my family to inform them that I could go home the next day if all went well through the night. If I kept improving with no setbacks, that was a good sign I would go home. She went on to say if my breathing was ok through the night, I was on my way home. The nurse explained they would also be observing me while I slept throughout the night to see how I was breathing while sleeping.

After the nurse left the room, I began to have a conversation with God. I sat up and said THANK YOU, JESUS!!! Surely, God, you did not bring me this far for me to have any type of setback. Surely you will allow me to make it through the night. I began to declare and decree in Jesus' name I would not have any breathing problems. I would rest and have a peaceful night. All my blood work would come back, showing I was well enough to go home.

I got up out of bed, barely able to walk and rolled the IV pole with me over to the windows and sat on the couch that was by the window. I looked out the window and spoke words into the atmosphere, "God, you are my Jehovah-Rapha-the Lord who heals."

The night came. I was so excited about the anticipation of going home. I actually took a shower, whereas I was just taking a sponge bath before. Talk about excitement!!! It seemed as if it was hours because I was moving extremely slow. But I was determined to let the water hit my entire body.

Philippians 4:13 (ISV) "I can do all things through him who strengthens me."

I proceeded to get in the bed. After laying a while, a test of faith came, my mind started thinking what-ifs again. Immediately I started shifting my thoughts. The word of God is sharper than a double edge sword. I began to think about true things. It's amazing what the Word of God will do with your mind when you start to recall what you have read and meditated on. I got a true revelation while in the hospital about staying ready. I started to drift off to sleep. The last thing I recall was waking up to bright sunshine coming through the window. Shortly after that, breakfast was delivered. When placing my breakfast on the cart by my bed, she said, "I didn't give you a menu for lunch. I was told you are going home today." I shouted, "Thank you, Jesus!!" She said, "Won't he do it?" I said, "God did it again!!

After she departed the room, I sat up and wept. I finally got myself together. I smiled and said out loud, "God, you bring me joy down in my soul."

1 Peter 5:7 (NIV) "Cast all your anxiety on him because he cares for you."

Breathe Moment

Holy Spirit reminded me my hospital stay was sent by God; therefore, God is the Alpha and Omega.

6

GOING HOME NEVER FELT SO GOOD

It was time to be released from the hospital. Oh, what a joyous day! I had been waiting for this day. I kept thinking to remain calm. It took most of the morning and part of the afternoon to get discharged. I started to get frustrated for a second, but the Holy Spirit reminded me to be anxious for nothing. My family had to travel about 3 hours to get to me.

Philippians 4:6-8 (NKJV) "Be anxious for nothing, but in everything by prayer and supplication, with thanksgiving, let our requests be made known to God; and the peace of God, which surpasses all understanding, will guard your hearts and minds through Christ Jesus."

God had already given me so much grace up to this point. Being the believer that I am, I continued to think and speak good thoughts while waiting. When we have to wait a little longer for things prayed for, and if we are not mindful of our thoughts, our mind starts to wander in the wrong direction, causing us to start complaining. I started speaking I am a conqueror. God did not bring me this far to leave me. He is with me and in control.

Psalm 31:24 (NIV) "Be strong and take heart, all you who hope in the Lord."

The doctor and nurse finally came into the room. The two of them were standing at a distance. She said Ms. Merchant, are you ready to go home? I just smiled and said, of course. The nurse smiled and said, we are overjoyed you are going home. The doctor said your family promised me they would take care of you once I release you. That is the only reason I am letting you go home because you can recover the rest of the time you need to heal at home. I had lost track of the days. I asked how many days I had been in the hospital, she said, "Five."

The doctor began to give me instructions:

- quarantine for 14 days

- drink lots of water

- take a shower, not a bath

- change my toothbrush daily

- take medications as prescribed

- call my primary doctor or the ER if I have any problems

- get lots of rest

The doctor and the nurse departed the room. Immediately the number "five" came back to my mind. I began to thank God. I recalled, according to the word of God, that "five" was the symbol of God's grace. God had shown me kindness and favor.

Job 23:10 (NIV) "But he knows the way that I take; when he tested me, I will come forth as gold."

I was so ready to go home. It seemed like it took my sisters forever to get from Alexandria to New Orleans. Finally, they had arrived. The nurse came to let me know and advised me someone would be coming with a wheelchair to take me down because no one was allowed to come into the hospital. I thanked her.

The assistant rolled the wheelchair to the door, and I had to walk to the door. She said her supervisor told her they were not to enter the rooms nor touch the patients. So, I took my time, barely able to walk. I made it to the wheelchair. The assistant proceeded to roll me towards the elevator.

The hospital was like a deserted town. All the doors were closed to patients' rooms. It was extremely cold. I had a dreary feeling to come upon me. There was no one walking the hallways. It reminded me of a scary movie I had seen. You know the movie where there is one person in the hallway, and no one else is in the entire hospital, and the person is trying to get out. Keep in mind this was during the very beginning of the pandemic. There were no people anywhere in the hospital. The only persons I saw were employees wearing scrubs, and they all were covered with protective gear.

As the assistant proceeded to roll me into the elevator, she pressed the button to go down. It was so, so cold. The elevator began to go down, and the noise was strange. I thought, "Girl, your mind is playing tricks with you." When you have been taking medications, your thinking can be unclear, so I assumed my mind was unclear at that moment.

The assistant said, "Your hair is pretty." I said, "Thank you." The doors to the elevator opened, and we were on the first floor. It was so quiet I thought I was in a strange place for a moment. The assistant proceeded to roll the wheelchair towards the exit door. She alerted the security that I was being released to a family member.

While I was being pushed to the door, the door opened, and all I saw was my sister Gisele standing in the door. I began to cry, and she began to say, "It's going to be ok, baby girl." I silently thanked God the entire time she lifted me up out of the wheelchair and assisted me into the car. She thanked the hospital staff, who brought me in the wheelchair. My other sisters were in the back, and all started saying, "God is good."

When I glanced in the back seat, their faces were so overjoyed. My sister, who was driving, had to take a second to get herself together to drive us to my apartment. We all joked and said, "Yes, get yourself together so we can make it safely."

We made it safely. My sisters made sure I made it to the bedroom and got in bed. That was where I would quarantine. I was so excited to be home! I just stared around the room, silently thanking God for his grace, for his love, for his healing power, for allowing me to defeat COVID-19.

Psalm 40: 1-3 (NIV) "I waited patiently for the Lord; he turned to me and heard me cry. He lifted me out of the slimy pit, out of the mud and mire; he set my feet on a rock and gave me a firm place to stand. He put a new song in my mouth, a hymn of praise to God. Many will see and fear and put their trust in the Lord."

I could hear my sisters conversations amongst themselves, seeming to be settling in. I eventually dozed off to sleep while praying. Sometime during the night, my sister woke me up to take medications.

Psalm 63:8 (ESV) "My soul clings to you; your right hand upholds me."

Breathe Moment

Let God worry-I am a firm believer. The Bible mentions 650 prayers because prayer takes sacrifice. Prayer is our shield for our soul, a powerful weapon against Satan, and is our source to walk through the process of the suffering.

7

GISELE -A SISTER'S LOVE

After getting a good night's rest, I woke up very early the next morning. I notice the daylight coming through the blinds. I opened my mouth up and said, "Thank you, God."

My sister Gisele came into the room. I noticed she had her mask and gloves on. I proceeded to put my mask on. It was as if she had designated herself as my caregiver.

Isaiah 54:10 (NIV) "Though the mountains be shaken, and the hills be removed, yet my unfailing love for you will not be shaken, nor my covenant of peace be removed, says the Lord, who has compassion on you."

Gisele did not hesitate when entering the room. There was no fear. God had already worked things out. She told me she and my other sisters had agreed she would stay and help me until I could do things for myself. My other sisters would go back home, and they would eventually rotate if needed.

She had prepared breakfast for me. So, she brought breakfast into the room along with liquids and medications that I needed to take. The thought of her catching COVID-19 didn't seem to be her concern. I mentioned it to her, and she said she had already prayed about it and had to trust God.

Job 33:6-7 (NIV) "I am just like you before God; I too have been made from clay. No fear of me should alarm you, nor should my hand be heavy upon you."

She left the room and closed the door; I began to cry and at the same time thank God for her willing heart. Fear began to set in my mind because she was putting her life in danger to take care of me. How do you handle fear of another's circumstances? I couldn't say go home because I could barely walk. I definitely could not prepare meals for myself. I could barely make it to the bathroom when needed. I could barely take a basic shower. Yet, I was concerned with us being in the same place. Holy Spirit reminded me of God bringing me this far. There was still part of his plan for me to continue to pray. I was called and anointed to pray for his people.

Romans 8:28 (AMP) "And we know with great confidence that God who is deeply concerned about us causes all things to work together as a plan for good for those who love God, to those who are called according to His plan and purpose."

I manage to keep my Bible, journal, devotional, and a couple of other books at the foot of the bed. These items and books gave me comfort. I could reach for them at any time I needed encouragement. This was one of those moments I really needed encouragement. Being in a room all alone tends to start working on your mind. So, I began to write out a prayer in my journal to God for myself and my sisters:

"God our Father, you are an amazing God. I am so grateful that you have put things in place for me to heal at home. Thank you for sending me my personal healing angel. Thank you for what you have done for me thus far. Thank you in advance for what you will do with the healing process you have already put into place. For that, I am grateful. Please cover my sisters from the crown of their heads to the sole of their feet. Keep the angels of protection surrounding them. I declare and decree in Jesus' name COVID-19 will not overtake their bodies. I ask that you keep their mind, body, soul, and spirit aligned with your will. God, I know you know what is best. You know what, why, how, and when for each of our lives. I

ask you to continue to heal my body and protect each of my sisters from all hurt, harm, and danger. Give those traveling back home grace. In Jesus' Name, AMEN."

I wrote a separate prayer for my sister Gisele because I had inquired about how my brother-in-law felt about her staying. As a Prayer Intercessor, I know the importance of praying specifics. I had already petitioned God to protect her from COVID-19. But the Holy Spirit prompted me to continue praying with specifics to totally release all the other concerns heavy on my heart. So, I picked my journal up and began to write:

"Lord, I ask that you prevent Gisele from getting overburdened while here taking care of me. Keep peace and harmony between her and her husband. Watch over him while she is away from home. Thank you for my brother-in-law, who is so agreeable with Gisele staying to take care of me. Thank you for her willing heart. This is a big sacrifice she is making on my behalf Lord. I praise you! Lord, I thank you! In Jesus' name, AMEN."

My other sisters stayed a few extra days and decided it was time for them to return to their homes. Each one of them individually came into the room to say their goodbyes. A sister's love was taught by our mother when we were very young. Our mother would always say be there for one another no matter what. Now don't get me wrong, we have our differences, but somehow, we are there when one is in need.

They all departed. That left me and my sister, Gisele, alone. She came to the room and said, "It's just me and you, baby girl, and God is going to take care of us both." I smiled. Something about the tone of her voice assured me she believed what she was speaking. Gisele said, "Don't you worry about anything; you just need to rest so you can heal." I responded, "Okay."

She went on to say she was going to establish somewhat of a schedule for my meals and medications since I had to quarantine for the next 14 days. With Gisele being the best cook in our family, I knew I was in good hands when it came to the meals. I thought, yes, God had worked it all out for my good. I smiled. Gisele left the room. Tears began to flow down my face. I quietly sobbed because I did not want to alarm her in any kind of way. I kept telling myself not to let her hear or know of my weeping moments. It seemed like the days were so long and the nights even longer. I would make a mark on my planner each day to keep a count of the 14 days.

You see, when you leave the hospital, the 14 days is just to make sure you don't infect someone else because your body is still fighting COVID-19. You are just at the stage where you don't need around-the-clock care. Those moments were between me and God. And if I tell you, there were so many of those moments. I tell you, oh how weeping is good for the body. Crying was not often for me unless I was really hurt. Usually, the hurt came after a lot of holding so much in. But at this point, holding in anything was not thought of. I was so heavy with all kinds of emotions that I realized crying was medicine to my soul.

Psalm 30:5 (NIV) "Weeping may remain for a night but rejoicing comes in the morning."

Each day thereafter, while healing, there were good days. There were some moments of darkness that seemed to overtake my mind. In fact, the devil would try and get me to doubt, oh but the Holy Spirit would remind me of the goodness of God. I would speak about how blessed I was. I began to truly realize how blessed I was. Not that I didn't know. But I really, really knew I was blessed. My body gave me proof that each day I woke up and saw the sun glomming through the window blind and feeling stronger each day.

Romans 12:12 (NIV) "Be joyful in hope, patient in affliction, faithful in prayer."

Having Gisele with me was nothing but the goodness of God. I was reminded of that each time she came into the room with a meal and to hear her say "Baby girl, it's time" for whatever it was time for — a meal, medications, or just peeping into the room asking me if I was okay. Sharing a word of encouragement or what she had read in her morning devotional. Even though I could not smell, my appetite was poor due to not being able to taste anything. Those times within the 14 days, I remained hopeful and stayed prayerful. God allowed me to see Gisele's braveness throughout the time she was caring for me. He allowed me to see he is the God of His Word.

2 Corinthians 1:3-4 (NIV) "Praise be to the God and Father of our Lord Jesus Christ, the Father of compassion and the God of all comfort, who comforts us in all our troubles, so that we can comfort those in any trouble with the comfort we ourselves have received from God."

Weeks had gone by. I was at the point where I could get around pretty good on my own. I was strong enough to walk alone and do things I needed to do personally for myself. I had several virtual appointments with the doctor just to see how I was coming along. It was time for Gisele to return back to her home. She had nursed me back to pretty good health. We had a conversation detailing what was needed to make sure I was clear prior to her leaving. I think this was to assure her that I would be ok. I assured her I would be ok, but I was somewhat nervous on the inside.

The night prior to her leaving, I dared not share with her how nervous I was. I knew at some point I would have to be alone and deal with continuing to heal. I had a restless night. I tossed and turned, and the what-ifs began to cloud my mind.

Proverbs 3:5 (NIV) "Trust in the Lord with all your heart and lean not on your own understanding; in all your ways acknowledge him, and he will make your paths straight."

I began to ask God, "Why?" Was that his way of testing me to see if I would totally rely on him? I learned over the years not to get preoccupied with the questions of why. God's reasons are often kept to Himself. He may hold them high above our understanding in order for us not to waver with our faith. I picked up my journal and began to write a prayer.

Matthew 11:28 (NLT) "Then Jesus said, "Come to me, all of you who are weary and carry heavy burdens, and I will give you rest."

_____

Breathe Moment

Your loved ones can carry your burdens along with you, share in the pain and suffering, but only God can lift the burdens.

8

THERAPY-WHO ME LORD?

It had been many, many weeks of being alone. I was not moving around like my normal self, but I could do enough to take my medications on time and prepare myself a meal whenever I became hungry. My appetite was not at its best due to still not being able to smell nor taste anything. I set a timer on my cell phone to remind me to eat something and take my medications. The doctor told me it was important to eat at least three meals a day, even if they were small meals.

At this point, virtual appointments were the only way to be seen by a physician. Besides, I definitely was not trying to go outside. The days seemed to go by quickly, but the nights seemed so long. It was partially due to me not sleeping through the night. Me not sleeping at night was causing me not to be able to heal. Lack of rest affects you mentally and physically. It definitely affects your immune system.

I began to feel my body going back to feeling how I felt when I first came home. I was extremely tired. I was going hours without eating. I began to tell myself something was not right due mainly to the way I was feeling. If you pay enough attention to your body, it will alert you when it's' in danger. I was restless, began to feel anxiety coming upon me. I began to tell myself, you just need to pray more. You just need to spend more time in the word of God. I began to search for scriptures related to restlessness and anxiety and write more prayers in my journal. I began to meditate on God's word even more.

Psalm 6:6 (NIV) "I am worn out from groaning; all night long I flood my bed with weeping and drench my couch with tears."

Psalm 6:2 (NIV) "Be merciful to me, LORD for I am faint; O LORD, heal me for my bones are in agony."

1 Peter 5:7 (NIV) "Cast all of your anxiety on him because he cares for you."

Psalm 20:1 (NIV) "May the Lord answer you when you are in distress; may the name of the God of Jacob protect you."

Prayer Moment-A cry out!!

God, I know you hear me. There is no doubt in my mind that you are a God that shall not lie. The way I am feeling and thinking right about now is neither good nor healthy for my mind, body, soul, and Spirit. I have studied your word, I have prayed, and prayed. Lord, I don't know what else to do. But I know I cannot continue to go on with sleepless nights and not give my body the proper nourishment to heal. I ask that you give me direction on what to do. I don't want to burden my family or friends. I don't want to seem like I am ungrateful for how far you have brought me up to this point. I see your people are still dying from COVID-19. The numbers are growing! God, surely you did not bring me this far for me to go backward. You are a God of grace and mercy. So, I ask you right now in the name of Jesus to show me or give me direction on what steps to take. I don't know what to do. I cry out to you! Lord, I am about to give up. I feel so lonely! I am so tired of the long dark nights. Help me, Lord! I pray this prayer to you, Lord. AMEN! AMEN! AMEN!

The Lord knows what it will take to get the roadblocks and hindrances out of the way. Sometimes in that process, things get shaken, but only to bring you to a place of fulfillment and joy! God's word assures us.

Ecclesiastes 3:11a (NIV), "He has made everything beautiful in its time."

At this point, I was desperate. Holy Spirit prompted me to contact my primary doctor. I had listened to the Holy Spirit the entire time throughout my COVID-19 encounter, and he not only helped save my life, but as far as I was concerned, he had not misled me. So, I went online into my hospital portal and wrote a request to my primary doctor. I wrote what I was experiencing and asked if there was anything she recommended. The nurse assistant responded within a couple of hours and said she would get back with me once she spoke with the doctor. It wasn't much of a time-lapse, and she responded by saying she would get me an appointment with someone who could help me. She went on to say someone from Able To would be contacting me. I went online and did some research about Able To. While reading about the agency, I saw the word therapist. Immediately I said to myself, I am not crazy. Then I thought, maybe I am losing my mind. I began to read more about the agency.

After reading about the agency, you know how we do- I began to have a conversation with God in my mind-Lord are you trying to tell me I am losing my mind? Is this you telling me I am crazy? I don't feel crazy. I just need help with not sleeping at night and anxiety that comes out of nowhere. I began to feel anxiety coming upon me and my breathing moving rapidly than normal. I began to breathe according to how I was taught when I was in the hospital. At that point, I became afraid. After calming myself down, I sat quietly. Thoughts going back and forth. Do I need a therapist? I was always in the belief that therapists were only for crazy people.

I had sat for about an hour. I had calmed myself down. I began to move around in the apartment to get my mind off of the therapist's ideal. I started doing things to keep my thoughts away from me possibly needing a therapist. Somehow the thought still would creep back into the forefront of my mind. I remained busy throughout the entire day. I even muzzled up the strength to cook myself a nice dinner.

It was time to go to bed. Got myself prepared for bed. I told myself to read one of the books at the foot of my bed to help me relax and fall asleep. I lost track of time after diving deep into the book I was reading, It's Okay Not to Be Okay: Moving Forward One Day at a Time by Sheila Walsh. This book was a blessing for me at a time I needed it. There was a scripture I highlighted in the book I would go back to often.

2 Corinthians 4:17-18 (NIV) "For our light and momentary troubles are achieving for us an eternal glory that far outweighs them all. So, we fix our eyes not on what is seen, but on what is unseen, since what is seen is temporary, but what is unseen is eternal."

It's amazing how God's words stand out specifically for what you need them for. At that time, I needed this verse for where I was within that night. I didn't go to bed with the therapist's question on my mind. Instead, I just said aloud, "Lord, I turn it all over to you."

I eventually drifted off to sleep. I was suddenly awakened. The Holy Spirit spoke to me and said, "You will be sent a helper; accept this person who is sent by God." I started crying because I knew it was God answering the thoughts I had about a therapist. The saying we often hear God answers our concerns in his timing is so true. God will wake you up and send the Holy Spirit when you least expect it. I knew it was God speaking because I was calm afterward and able to fall peacefully back to sleep. I slept all through the night. When I woke up, I could feel a sense of calmness all over my body. That, too, was a confirmation I had heard from God.

Several days went by. I received an email from the agency the doctor had recommended. It required me to answer a series of questions. I started not to complete the questionnaire. Once again, the Holy Spirit prompted me to complete the questionnaire. I proceeded to complete the questionnaire. I didn't concern myself with the idea of a therapist. I thought, "God will work things out."

Philippians 4:11-13 (NIV) "I am not saying this because I am in need, for I have learned to be content whatever the circumstances. I know what is to be in need, and I know what it is to have plenty. I have learned the secret of being content in any and every situation, whether well fed or hungry, whether living in plenty or in want. I can do everything through him who gives me strength."

Within several days of completing the questionnaire, there was a call coming in on my cell phone. I didn't recognize the number. Normally I wouldn't answer such calls, but the Holy Spirit prompted me again to answer. I proceeded to answer the call. The voice on the other end of the call. My Jesus!! A Therapist!! She immediately introduced herself and informed me where she was calling from. She went on to say her agency assigned her to me, and she was reaching out to see how she could assist me. Her voice, her tone, and her words were all God. ALL!! This call set things in motion.

I was in no way reluctant to start sharing with her the things I was experiencing. It was as if the river of release started to flow like a rushing river. I don't think I took a breather while sharing all the things I was experiencing. I began to weep to the point I was gasping to breathe. I started apologizing for crying. She said, "You don't have to apologize for crying. It's good for the soul." She just listened and allowed me to speak. Finally, I was able to calm down. She said, "You have been through a traumatic experience. The things you are sharing with me are not abnormal." She went on to discuss the process and asked, "What would be a good time for us to continue the sessions?" We agreed upon a day and time. It's amazing how quickly an hour can go by when you are in therapy. She went on to share with me that a nutritionist would also be contacting me; the two of them worked as a team.

After the call ended, I immediately fell on my knees, started praising and thanking God for answering my need. Immediately, the Holy Spirit reminded me that God answered my cry and sent me the assistance I needed. "Jesus!!"

Yes, I am SOLD OUT TO PRAYER!!

Psalm 121:1-2 (KJV) **"I will lift up mine eyes unto the hills, From whence cometh my help. My help cometh from the LORD, which made heaven and earth."**

Breathe Moment

God is the only one who can give you a sense of hope in a time of suffering.

9

SUFFERING TO A TROPHY OF GRACE

There is never suffering without an ending. The obstacles encountered are placed before you for a purpose. Gods' lessons of grace could only be learned in the depths of pain and suffering. God tests faith, patience, endurance, and most of all, trusting him.

Even though you are brought and put into a very low position, there is always a special blessing. That special blessing can also be looked at as divine favor. God is in charge of all things. Even the traumatic aftermath of the suffering. We have His Word to take comfort in knowing that God does not allow suffering in our lives that is too great for us to bear. When we walk in difficult places, God sends the strength and nourishment we need to face what comes our way, not all at once but day by day.

At times we may forget his faithfulness to us. When trials and tests come, it may seem as if God has surely forgotten us. When friends fail us and our lives fall apart, we may feel he has forsaken us. Yet he is the One, the faithful God, on whom we can depend, who will never let us down.

1 Peter 5:10 (ESV) "And after you have suffered a little while, the God of all grace, who has called you to his eternal glory in Christ, will himself restore, confirm, strengthen, and establish you."

You may wonder why I consider myself a "Trophy of Grace." The memorable endurance I will forever carry within my heart is God, and God alone is enough for all my soul needs. Gods' dealings with us are meant to teach us God is enough. Sometimes God takes us through suffering to show us even during those times in our lives, his grace is sufficient. Regardless of the way God chooses to do so, we can trust him as our ever-present guide.

John 1:16 (NIV) "From the fullness of his grace we have all received one blessing after another."

We must take a good look within ourselves. Sure, we may ask whether we deserve the suffering. It is God's grace.

Romans 3:24 (NIV) "And are justified freely by his grace through the redemption that came by Christ Jesus."

It means God never takes away except to give us back something better. We must be determined enough to walk through the process, which requires waiting, embracing the suffering, not resenting it, for it often takes God time to turn a painful situation into good.

As I close the ENCOUNTER with COVID-19, This is my prayer:

God, thank You! Shouting from the top of my lungs and the core of my heart for your healing grace, your saving grace, your AMAZING GRACE, choosing me as your "Trophy of Grace," to share there is "Life after The Encounter with COVID-19." In Jesus Name, AMEN!!!

Exodus 12:14 (MSG) "This will be a Memorial Day for you; you will celebrate it as a festival to God down through the generations, a fixed festival celebration to be always observed."

A Final Breathe Moment

I don't place any value on my own life. I want to finish the race I'm running that has been put before me. I want to carry out the mission I received from the Lord Jesus-the mission of testifying to the Good News of God's GRACE.

A Prayer for those who lost loved ones to COVID-19:

GOD, I come to You humbly, thanking You for the people who will read this book. I pray you allow them to have their moments with a receptive heart. I pray their pain is for short moments. Let the Holy Spirit remind them to count their blessings and strengthen their individual prayer lives. I pray your words will give them peace in every way possible. Allow this prayer to encourage each of them, personally, professionally, and especially spiritually. Let them continually feel your love. Give them strength to turn all their feelings over to you and to especially know you are ALWAYS A GOOD GOD.

God, I thank you for the power of PRAYER.

In Jesus Name AMEN

Acknowledgments

To Jehovah-Rapha, The God Who Heals-My Healer.

Special Acknowledgement to my sister, Gisele Samuel, who willingly accepted the call from God with his protection to nurse me back to health. God sent you when I was at my lowest. I will forever be grateful!

To my family near and far, thank you for your support and prayers.

To Charlain Hubbard-a true friend you are-you took a chance and came to my rescue in a much-needed time. You are a keepsake!

To My, Therapists-God sent you all into my life at the time He knew you would be the one to help me realize my life was not over. The therapy sessions, along with your prayers led by God, I am grateful you obeyed his leading.

To my friends who prayed with me and for me and those who sent words of encouragement, I am grateful.

ABOUT THE AUTHOR

Anita Johnson Merchant, known as "The Prayer Advocate," is a Certified Prayer Intercessor whose motto is, "I am SOLD OUT TO PRAYER." She is an Honor Graduate of the 2014 God's Leading Lady-Life Enrichment Program at The Potter's House of Dallas, Texas. She recently retired after 30 years of service from the Social Security Administration. She is the mother of two sons and grandmother of a little girl sent from heaven. She knows the power of prayer from living through her encounter, where prayer was the one thing that helped her survive. Her passion for prayer has led her to a mission of prayer being at the forefront of daily living. She is the founder of the ministry Visuals of Prayer #7, in which she teaches the signature program "The Prayer Incubator." She is the author of *Strength of a Prayer Intercessor.* Her mission is to educate, equip, and encourage how to establish and maintain a consistent prayer life. Anita Johnson Merchant's motto is "Let nothing good or bad interrupt your consistent prayer life." To learn more about Anita Johnson Merchant, visit www.anitamerchant.com

Made in the USA
Middletown, DE
17 April 2022